DUMP Dinners

DUMP Dinners

Amazingly Easy and Delicious Dump Recipes

Julia Grady

Dylanna Press

Contents

1

What Are Dump Dinners?

WHILE THE NAME MIGHT not be appealing, the idea of preparing delicious meals without a lot of fuss certainly is. The name comes from the idea that the ingredients can simply be "dumped" into a casserole dish or slow cooker and then cooked. Most dump dinners can also be frozen in freezer bags and then just popped in the oven, pot, or slow cooker when needed.

Dump dinners actually have a long history and were popular additions to many pot-luck dinners in the seventies and eighties. Today, they are once again popular for providing home-cooked meals without a lot of fuss.

Why We Love Dump Dinners

With the hectic pace of today's lifestyles getting dinner on the table every night is no easy task. When pressed for time, dump dinners make the perfect solution to the question, What's for dinner?

Dump dinners are so popular because they are so easy to make. These recipes feature simple ingredients that you probably already have on hand in your freezer, refrigerator, and pantry. They do not require complicated cooking techniques or that you stand over the stove, stirring and sautéing. The majority of the recipes are mixed right in the pan they are cooked in, with the added bonus of saving cleanup time.

This book contains the best dump dinner recipes around. None of these recipes take more than 15 minutes of hands-on time to prepare, and most a lot less. When you're short on time, you can turn to any one of these delicious recipes and have a home-cooked meal on the table with little effort and big rewards.

The recipes in this book can be cooked in several ways:

- Baked in the oven
- Cooked in a slow cooker

- Cooked on the stovetop
- Microwaved
- Frozen and cooked later

So whether you'd like to throw something in the slow cooker and come home hours later to an aromatic meal or pop a quickly prepared casserole into the oven, you are sure to find a recipe you and your family will love.

Stocking Your Kitchen

A big part of preparing meals without a lot of fuss is having the ingredients you need on hand. Keeping your pantry stocked with a few essentials will go a long way toward making it easy to prepare a quick and healthy meal.

Pantry Items

- Applesauce, unsweetened
- Baking powder and baking soda
- Beans (dried and/or canned)
- Beef broth
- Black beans
- Bread crumbs
- Brown rice
- Brown sugar
- Chicken broth
- Condensed milk
- Corn, canned
- Cornstarch or arrowroot
- Dried fruit and nuts
- Evaporated milk
- Flour (unbleached and whole wheat)
- Herbs – basil, oregano, parsley, rosemary, sage, thyme, etc.
- Honey
- Hot sauce
- Lentils
- Maple syrup
- Marinades
- Nuts
- Oatmeal

- Olive and canola oils
- Pasta in various shapes
- Peanut butter
- Quinoa
- Rice
- Salad dressing
- Salsa
- Salt
- Soy sauce
- Spices – cayenne pepper, chili powder, cinnamon, coriander, cumin, paprika, turmeric, etc.
- Sugar
- Tomato sauce
- Tomatoes, canned
- Tuna packed in water
- Vegetable broth
- Vegetable oil spray
- Vinegar (apple cider, balsamic, white wine)

Refrigerator Items

- Bottled lemon juice
- Butter
- Cheese – various types, shredded
- Cottage cheese
- Dijon mustard
- Eggs and/or egg substitute
- Fresh fruit
- Fresh vegetables
- Fresh-pack salad greens
- Garlic
- Ketchup
- Lemons
- Lime
- Low-fat and nonfat yogurt
- Mayonnaise
- Milk
- Natural peanut butter
- Onions
- Peanut butter
- Potatoes
- Salad dressings

- Tortillas, whole wheat or corn
- Yogurt

Freezer Items

- Chicken
- Fish
- Frozen fruit
- Frozen vegetables
- Ground beef
- Pork
- Sausage
- Shrimp

Tips for Cooking Quick Meals

There are a couple of things you can do to make it easier on yourself when it comes to preparing quick, healthy, and great-tasting meals for you and your family.

Use precooked meats. Rotisserie chicken and turkey are great to have on hand for adding to recipes that call for precooked meat. You can also buy cooked, seasoned grilled chicken strips, cooked shrimp, and cooked beef strips in most supermarkets.

Prepare double and triple batches. When cooking it is often just as easy to double or even triple the recipe. Store the extras in freezer bags and pull one out to defrost whenever you need a quick meal.

Make use of the microwave. The microwave can be a real lifesaver for those times when you forget to take a meal out of the freezer to defrost. Just pop it in, hit defrost, and in minutes you are ready to go. You can also use the microwave for cooking entire meals.

Keep flavorful items on hand. Cranking up the flavor factor is easy when your pantry is well-stocked with items such as flavored salsas, pesto, capers, roasted tomatoes, and hot sauce.

Buy prepared vegetables. Yes, buying precut broccoli, onions, or cauliflower will cost you a bit more. But the time savings and lack of waste may more than make up for it when you want to whip together a quick meal without having to dice and chop.

Use bottled sauces, dressings, and marinades. You don't have to feel guilty about not making your own homemade sauces or dressings. There are so many great-tasting and convenient options available now that this is really a no-brainer when it comes to saving time in the kitchen. Keep your pantry stocked with jars of flavorful pasta sauces, salad dressings, and marinades.

2

Soups

CHEESY TORTELLINI SOUP

Servings: 6

This easy and delicious soup is hearty enough to be a main course.
Serve with crusty bread to sop up the flavorful broth.

1 pound ground beef

1 (28 ounce) can crushed tomatoes

1 (15 ounce) jar tomato sauce

2 cups beef broth

1 cup water

1 teaspoon ground basil

1 teaspoon ground oregano

Salt and freshly ground black pepper, to taste

1 can sliced mushrooms

1 cup fresh spinach, roughly chopped

1 (8 ounce) package cheese tortellini

1 cup mozzarella cheese, shredded

1.   In a large pot, brown beef over medium heat. Drain, keeping beef in pot. Add tomatoes, tomato sauce, broth, water, basil, oregano, salt, pepper, mushrooms, spinach, and tortellini.

2.   Bring to a boil, reduce heat, and simmer for 15 minutes.

3.   Serve topped with shredded cheese.

Tip: This can also be prepared in a slow cooker. Add all ingredients except for spinach and cheese. Cover and cook on low for 6-7 hours or high for 4-5 hours. Add spinach during last 20 minutes of cooking.

EASY TACO SOUP

Servings: 6
This chili-like soup uses canned vegetables and taco seasoning.
It has great taste and is a snap to prepare.

1 (15 ounce) can diced tomatoes
1 (15 ounce) can beef chili
1 (15 ounce) can kidney beans, drained and rinsed
1 (15 ounce) can corn
1 (15 ounce) can tomato sauce
1 packet taco seasoning
2 cups water
1 cup cheddar cheese, shredded

In a slow cooker: Dump all ingredients except for cheese into slow cooker. Cover and cook on low for 4 hours. Serve topped with shredded cheese.

On the stove top: Dump all ingredients in large saucepan. Cover, bring to boil, reduce heat and simmer for 25 minutes. Serve topped with shredded cheese.

HAMBURGER SOUP

Servings: 6-8

This soup is good and hearty. Full of vegetables, it is a meal in itself.

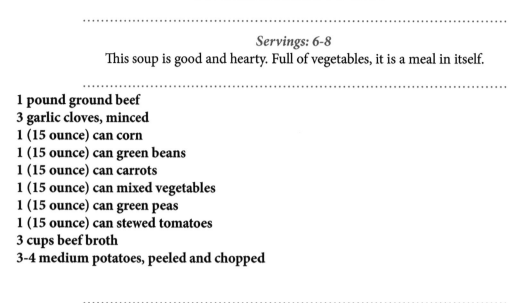

1 pound ground beef
3 garlic cloves, minced
1 (15 ounce) can corn
1 (15 ounce) can green beans
1 (15 ounce) can carrots
1 (15 ounce) can mixed vegetables
1 (15 ounce) can green peas
1 (15 ounce) can stewed tomatoes
3 cups beef broth
3-4 medium potatoes, peeled and chopped

On the stovetop: Heat large pot over medium heat. Add beef and cook until browned. Add garlic and cook for 2-3 minutes. Add all remaining ingredients to pot. Stir to mix. Bring to boil, reduce heat, cover and simmer for one hour.

In the slow cooker: Brown beef and garlic as above. Add to slow cooker along with all other ingredients. Cover and cook on high for 3-4 hours or low for 5-6 hours.

CHICKEN NOODLE SOUP

....

Servings: 8

Nothing is more soothing than home-cooked chicken noodle soup.

....

2 pounds chicken, skinless and boneless, cut into 2" pieces
6 cups low-sodium chicken broth
1/2 teaspoon crushed red pepper flakes
1 cup celery, diced
4 carrots, sliced
1 small onion, diced
3 cloves garlic, minced
1/4 cup fresh, chopped, Italian parsley
1/2 teaspoon black pepper
Pinch sea salt
8 ounces whole wheat noodles

....

1.   Add all ingredients, except the noodles, to the slow cooker and cook for 6-8 hours on low, or until carrots are tender.
2.   The last hour of cooking time, add in the noodles and continue cooking one additional hour or until pasta is to desired doneness.

Note: This soup can also be prepared on the stovetop. Add all ingredients except for noodles to large pot. Bring to a boil, reduce heat, cover and let simmer for 30 minutes. Add noodles and cook for another 15-20 minutes.

BLACK BEAN SOUP

Servings: 4

This is a flavorful and very easy soup to make.
Get creative with additional toppings such as crispy tortilla tips, chopped green onion, cilantro, diced avocado, even a spoonful of cooked rice.

· ·

3 cups chicken or beef broth
1 small onion, chopped
3 (15 ounce) cans black beans, rinsed and drained
1 cup salsa
1 teaspoon cumin
½ teaspoon cayenne pepper
Salt and freshly ground black pepper, to taste
Sour cream, for topping (optional)
Cheddar cheese, shredded for topping (optional)

· ·

1.   In a large saucepan, combine broth and onions, bring to boil. Reduce heat and simmer for 5 minutes, until onions are tender.
2.   In a bowl, mash one can of beans with a potato masher. Add salsa, cumin, cayenne pepper, salt, and black pepper. Mix to combine.
3.   Add 2 cans black beans plus the seasoned mashed beans to the broth. Stir, reduce heat to low, and simmer for 30 minutes.
4.   Serve topped with sour cream or shredded cheese, or both!

Note: This soup also works wonderfully in the slow cooker. Prepare as directed, adding every-thing into the slow cooker. Cover, and cook on low for 6-7 hours or high for 3-4 hours.

SOUTHWESTERN CHICKEN SOUP

Servings: 8
This is a nutritious soup that is colorful and flavorful.

1 tablespoon olive oil
1 pound chicken breasts, chopped into bite-size pieces
1 small onion, chopped
3 cloves garlic, chopped
1 can chili peppers, chopped
1 tablespoon cumin
1 jar salsa
4 cups chicken stock
2 limes, juiced
1 14-oz can pinto or black beans, drained and rinsed
1 pouch microwaveable ready rice (or two cups cooked rice)
1 cup shredded cheddar cheese
¼ cup cilantro, torn

1.   Heat oil in large pot over medium-high heat. Add chicken, onions, and garlic and cook for 3-4 minutes. Add remaining ingredients except for cheese and cilantro, stir well to combine. Simmer for 15 minutes.
2.   Serve topped with cheese and cilantro.

HEARTY MINESTRONE SOUP

Servings: 8

This soup provides a nice vegetarian dinner. Serve with some crusty whole-grain bread.

4 cups tomato juice, low-sodium
4 cups vegetable broth, low-sodium
1 medium onion, chopped
4 cloves garlic, diced
3 stalks celery, diced
3 large carrots, sliced
2 medium zucchini, chopped
1 red pepper, diced
1 (15 ounce) can white beans, rinsed and drained
1 cup dried Stelline pasta (can substitute orzo, farfalline, or other small pasta)
2 teaspoons dried basil
2 teaspoons dried oregano
Freshly ground black pepper, to taste

In the slow cooker: Place all ingredients into slow cooker. Cover, and cook on low for 8-9 hours or high for 4-5 hours, until vegetables are tender.

On the stove top: Place all ingredients into large pot. Cover, bring to a boil, reduce heat and simmer for about an hour, until vegetables are tender.

FIVE-CAN DUMP SOUP

Servings: 8
This soup will be ready to eat in literally five minutes.

1 (14.4-ounce) can fat-free chicken broth
1 (14.4-ounce) can corn, drained and rinsed
1 (14.4-ounce) can black beans, drained and rinsed
1 (14.4-ounce) can fat-free refried beans
1 (14.4-ounce) can no-salt added diced tomatoes

1.   Combine all ingredients in saucepan. Mix well to combine. Simmer for 5 minutes until heated through.

Note: Garnish with sour cream, shredded cheese, avocado, or green onions.

3

Chicken Recipes

CREAMY CHICKEN AND CHEESE BAKE

Servings: 6

2 (10.75 ounce) cans cream of chicken soup
8 ounces plain yogurt
1 3/4 cups milk, divided
2 pounds cooked chicken, cut into 1-inch chunks
1/2 teaspoon salt
1 teaspoon freshly ground black pepper
3/4 cup Bisquick
1/4 cup cornmeal
1 egg
1 cup cheddar cheese, shredded

1.   Preheat oven to 375 degrees F.
2.   In a large casserole dish, stir together soup, yogurt, and 1 cup milk. Mix well.
3.   Add chicken, salt, and pepper and mix well.
4.   In a bowl, mix together Bisquick, cornmeal, egg, and remaining milk. Pour over chicken mixture and mix gently to combine. Sprinkle with cheese.
5.   Baked, uncovered, for 30-35 minutes or until cheese is golden brown.

SALSA DUMP CHICKEN

....

Servings: 4

This is a good one to make up in advance and keep frozen in the freezer. Just pull it out and heat.

....

1 1/2 pounds chicken pieces
1 (12 ounce) jar salsa
1 (1.25 ounce) package taco seasoning
1 cup apricot jam

....

1.   Preheat oven to 350 degrees F.
2.   Place all ingredients into large baking dish. Mix to coat chicken.
3.   Bake for 30-45 minutes, or until chicken juices run clear.

Note: Can also be cooked in the slow cooker. Put all ingredients in slow cooker, mix, cover, and cook on low for 7-8 hours.

CHICKEN CURRY

Servings: 6

This chicken recipe is spicy and delicious.

2 pounds chicken parts, skinless, quartered
3/4 cup coconut milk
1 cup chicken broth
2 tablespoon tomato paste
3 garlic cloves, minced
1 tablespoon ground ginger
6 tablespoon curry powder
2 bell peppers, chopped
1 yellow onion, thinly sliced
salt and pepper, to taste
1 dash red pepper flakes

In a slow cooker: Combine all ingredients, except for the chicken. Mix well to blend. Add the chicken; ensure that all pieces are totally submerged in the liquid. Cover and cook on low setting for about 7 hours or on high setting for about 5 hours.

In the oven: Combine all ingredients, except for chicken, in casserole dish. Mix well to blend. Add the chicken, ensure that all pieces are submerged in the liquid. Cover and cook in 375 degree F oven for 45 minutes or until chicken is cooked through.

PESTO CHICKEN

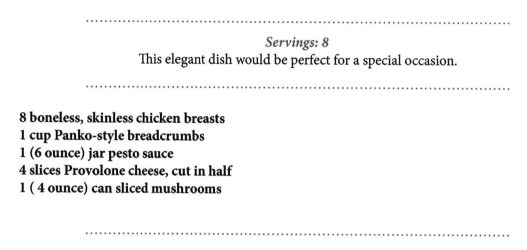

Servings: 8
This elegant dish would be perfect for a special occasion.

8 boneless, skinless chicken breasts
1 cup Panko-style breadcrumbs
1 (6 ounce) jar pesto sauce
4 slices Provolone cheese, cut in half
1 (4 ounce) can sliced mushrooms

1.   Preheat oven to 350 degrees F.
2.   Spray 9 x 13 baking dish with cooking spray.
3.   Place bread crumbs in shallow bowl. Coat chicken breasts in breadcrumbs and place in baking dish.
4.   Spread pesto sauce evenly over chicken breasts. Top with ½ slice Provolone cheese. Top with mushrooms.
5.   Bake for 45 minutes or until chicken is cooked through.

Note: Serve over pasta.

PINEAPPLE CHICKEN

Servings: 4-6

1 pound chicken tenders or chicken breasts
1 medium onion, chopped
3 tablespoons olive oil
1/2 cup ketchup
2 teaspoons dry mustard
1 (8 ounce) can crushed pineapple
Pinch of salt
1 tablespoon chili sauce (optional)

1. Preheat oven to 350 degrees F.
2. Add all ingredients to large baking dish or casserole. Mix gently to coat chicken.
3. Bake, uncovered for 20-30 minutes, or until chicken is cooked through and juices run clear.
4. Serve with rice.

Note: This could also be cooked in a slow cooker. Just put all ingredients in slow cooker, cover, and cook on low for 6-8 hours or high for 4-5 hours.

CHICKEN ENCHILADA BAKE

....

Servings: 6-8
This is a cheesy dish that is sure to be a crowd pleaser.

....

4 cups cooked chicken, cut into bites-size pieces
2 cans cream of chicken soup
3 cups shredded Mexican cheese, divided
1 (1o ounce) can chopped tomatoes and green chilies
1 can green chilies
1/4 cup fresh cilantro, chopped
4 large flour tortillas
1 cup corn, fresh or frozen
1 (15 ounce) can black beans, rinsed and drained
Optional toppings: chopped tomatoes, salsa, sour cream, avocado slices

....

1. Preheat oven to 350 degrees F.
2. Mix together chicken, soup, 1 cup shredded cheese, tomatoes, and cilantro.
3. Spray large casserole dish with cooking spray.
4. Add 1 cup of filling to bottom of casserole, spread evenly.
5. Next, later ingredients on top: tortilla, 2 cups filling, corn, beans, tortilla, 2 cups filling, corn, beans, tortilla. Top with shredded cheese.
6. Cover with aluminum foil and bake for 20 minutes. Uncover and bake for an addition 15 minutes or until cheese is golden brown and casserole is heated through.

CREAMY CHICKEN AND BISCUIT CASSEROLE

Servings: 6

This is a very easy comfort food dish that your family is sure to love.

2 pounds boneless chicken breast, chopped
1 small onion, chopped
1 (10.75 ounce) can cream of chicken soup
1/2 cup sour cream
1 cup milk
1 bag frozen mixed vegetables
1 1/2 cups cheddar cheese, shredded
1 package biscuits

1.   Preheat oven to 350 degrees F.
2.   Spray 11 x7 casserole dish with cooking spray.
3.   Combine chicken, onion, soup, sour cream, milk, and vegetables in bowl. Spread evenly into prepared baking dish. Sprinkle half of shredded cheese over mixture.
4.   Bake in oven for 15 minutes. Remove from oven and arrange biscuits in single layer over casserole. Sprinkle with remaining cheese.
5.   Return to oven and cook for an additional 20 minutes or until golden brown.

BLACK BEAN CHICKEN

Servings: 6

This is a very simple recipe but it is very tasty.

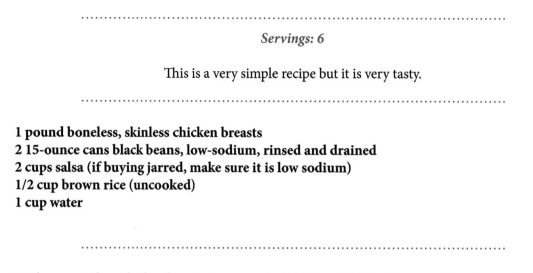

1 pound boneless, skinless chicken breasts
2 15-ounce cans black beans, low-sodium, rinsed and drained
2 cups salsa (if buying jarred, make sure it is low sodium)
1/2 cup brown rice (uncooked)
1 cup water

In the oven: Place chicken breasts in casserole dish. Top with black beans, salsa, rice, and water. Stir to mix. Cover and bake in 375 degree F oven for 45 minutes, or until chicken is cooked through.

In the slow cooker: Place chicken breasts in slow cooker. Pour beans, rice, water, and salsa over chicken. Stir to combine. Cover and cook on low for 8-10 hours.

SPANISH CHICKEN AND RICE

Servings: 4

2 tablespoons olive oil
2 pounds chicken thighs, boneless and skinless
1 pound chorizo sausage, sliced
1 medium yellow onion, diced
1 red pepper, chopped
4 garlic cloves, minced
1 cup long-grain white rice, uncooked
2 cups chicken stock
1 (15 ounce) can diced tomatoes
1 teaspoon paprika
1 teaspoon thyme
¼ cup black olives, pitted

1.   Heat olive oil in large pot over medium heat. Add chicken pieces and sausage and brown for 4-5 minutes. Add onion, pepper, and garlic and sauté for another 2-3 minutes.
2.   Add rice, stock, tomatoes, paprika, and thyme, stir well. Cover and simmer on low heat for 45 minutes, until chicken is cooked and rice has absorbed liquid.
3.   Add olives, mix, and serve.

GARLICKY LEMON CHICKEN WITH CAPERS

Servings: 4 to 6

1 pound chicken tenders or chicken breasts, boneless
3 cloves garlic
1/4 cup extra-virgin olive oil
Juice of 1 lemon
1 tablespoon parsley
3 tablespoons capers
Salt and freshly ground pepper to taste

1.   Preheat oven to 350 degrees F.
2.   Mix together all ingredients in a large bowl. Stir to thoroughly coat chicken. Alternatively, place in large zipper lock bag and shake.
3.   Pour chicken and marinade into baking dish.
4.   Cook for 25-30 minutes until chicken is cooked through and juices run clear.
5.   Serve over pasta.

CHICKEN AND RICE CASSEROLE

....

Servings: 4

....

4 chicken breasts, cut into 1-2 inch chunks
1 1/2 cups rice, uncooked
2 1/2 cups chicken broth
1 package onion soup mix

....

1.   Preheat oven to 400 degrees F.
2.   Add all ingredients to 9 x 13 baking dish. Mix well to combine.
3.   Cover with foil and bake for 40-45 minutes or until chicken is cooked through.

PROVENCAL CHICKEN AND WHITE BEANS

....

Servings: 6

Another very easy recipe that tastes like you spent a lot of time in the kitchen.

....

1 1/2 pounds chicken breast, boneless and skinless
1 red bell pepper, diced
1 (16 ounce) can cannellini beans, low sodium, rinsed and drained
1 (14.5 ounce) can diced tomatoes, no salt added
1/4 teaspoon salt
1/2 teaspoon freshly ground black pepper
2 teaspoons basil
2 teaspoons oregano
1 teaspoon thyme

....

In the slow cooker: Place all ingredients in slow cooker. Stir, cover, and cook on low for 7-8 hours.

In the oven: Place all ingredients into casserole dish. Stir, cover, and bake in 375 degree F oven for 45 minutes, or until chicken is cooked through.

CHICKEN AND RICE CASSEROLE II

Servings: 4

Another version of this versatile dish! Great for leftovers chicken.

3 tablespoons butter
3 tablespoons flour
1 teaspoon dried thyme
1 cup chicken broth
1 cup milk
2 cups diced cooked chicken
3/4 cup frozen peas, thawed
1/4 teaspoon salt
1/8 teaspoon black pepper
2 cups cooked rice
¼ cup dry breadcrumbs
1 tablespoon grated parmesan cheese

1. Preheat oven to 400 degrees F.
2. Melt 3 tablespoons of butter in a saucepan over medium heat, whisk in flour and thyme and cook for 1 minute.
3. Gradually stir in broth and milk, until smooth.
4. Stir in chicken and peas and season with salt and pepper. Remove from heat.
5. Spread rice in bottom of baking dish, pour creamed chicken mixture over rice.
6. Sprinkle with bread crumbs and Parmesan cheese.
7. Bake for 20-25 minutes until heated through and bubbly.

CHICKEN, BROCCOLI, AND RICE BAKE

....

Servings: 6

....

4 chicken breasts, boneless and skinless, cut into 1-2 inch pieces
1 bag broccoli florets (fresh or frozen)
1 1/2 cups rice, uncooked
1 can cream of mushroom soup
2 1/2 cups chicken broth
1 teaspoon garlic powder
Salt and freshly ground black pepper, to taste
½ cup crushed Ritz cracker crumbs

....

1.   Preheat oven to 375 degrees F.
2.   Place all ingredients except for cracker crumbs into large baking dish. Stir to combine.
Sprinkle with cracker crumbs.
3.   Cover and cook for 40-45 minutes or until chicken is cooked through.

WHITE CHICKEN CHILI

Servings: 6

2 (15 ounce) cans white beans (Great Northern or cannellini), no-salt added
1 pound chicken, boneless and skinless, cut into chunks
1 (15 ounce) can diced tomatoes, no salt added
1 (4.5 ounce) can green chilies, drained and chopped
1 medium yellow onion, chopped
3 cloves garlic, minced
1 tablespoon chili powder
1 teaspoon cumin
1 teaspoon oregano
1 teaspoon cayenne pepper

In the slow cooker: Add all ingredients to slow cooker. Stir to combine, cover and cook on low for 8 hours or high for 4 hours.

On the stovetop: Add all ingredients to large pot. Stir to combine, cover, and simmer for 45 minutes or until chicken is cooked through.

4

Pork Recipes

HONEY-GINGER PORK CHOPS

Servings: 6

These pork chops are very flavorful. Could also be cooked on the grill.

6 boneless pork chops
¼ cup cider vinegar
½ cup honey
2 cloves garlic, minced
½ teaspoon ground ginger
2 tablespoons soy sauce
½ teaspoon freshly ground black pepper

1.   In a bowl, combine all ingredients except pork chops.
2.   Pour into large zipper lock bag and add pork chops. Seal and shake to coat pork chops. Place in refrigerator for a minimum of 1 hour.
3.   Pour pork chops and marinade into baking dish. Cook in 350 degree F oven for 35-40 minutes or until pork reaches internal temperature of 160 degrees.

SLOW COOKED PORK WITH PINEAPPLE

....

Servings: 8

This pork comes out very tender. The leftovers make great sandwiches.

....

1 (15 ounce) can crushed pineapple, undrained
3/4 cup barbecue sauce
1/2 cup chili sauce
2 teaspoons dried Italian seasoning
½ teaspoon garlic powder
1/2 teaspoon salt
1/4 teaspoon ground black pepper
1 (2 pound) boneless pork loin roast

....

1.   Place all ingredients into slow cooker. Cover and cook on high for 4 to 5 hours or low for 6 to 8 hours.

EASY LENTIL AND KIELBASA STEW

Servings: 4

1 cup dry lentils
1 pound kielbasa, cut into slices
4 cups chicken broth
1 (15 ounce) can diced tomatoes
1 large potato, peeled and chopped
2 carrots, chopped
1 onion, chopped
2 celery stalks, chopped
1 tablespoon dried parsley
1 tablespoon dried basil
1 garlic clove, minced
Freshly ground black pepper, to taste

1.   Rinse the lentils and drain.
2.   In a large saucepan combine all ingredients. Stir to mix.
3.   Bring to a boil, cover, reduce heat and simmer for 45 minutes or until lentils and vegetables are tender.

SAUSAGE AND PEPPERONI PIZZA CASSEROLE

Servings: 10-12

3 cups marinara sauce (jarred or homemade)
1 pound ground turkey sausage
1 small onion, chopped
1 medium green pepper, chopped
6 ounces pepperoni
1 cup mushrooms, sliced
1 package wheat biscuits (i.e., Pillsbury), cut into quarters
2 cups mozzarella cheese, shredded

1. Preheat oven to 350 degrees F.
2. Heat skillet over medium heat, add sausage and cook until browned.
3. Combine all ingredients except cheese in a bowl.
4. Pour into 9 x 13 baking dish. Sprinkle cheese on top.
5. Bake uncovered for 30 minutes or until cheese is golden brown.

ITALIAN SAUSAGE CASSEROLE

Servings: 4

Easy and economical one-dish meal.

1 pound Italian sausages, casings removed
4 medium potatoes, peeled and cubed
2 large carrots, sliced
1 medium yellow onions, chopped
2 (15 ounce cans) seasoned chopped tomatoes
1 teaspoon sea salt
1 teaspoon freshly ground black pepper
1/2 teaspoon dried oregano
1/2 teaspoon garlic powder

1.   Preheat oven to 375 degrees F.
2.   Cut sausage into 1-inch pieces. Place in large casserole dish.
3.   Add potatoes, carrots, and onions over sausage. Pour chopped tomatoes on top. Season with salt, pepper, and oregano.
4.   Cover and bake for an hour and 20 minutes. Uncover for last 15 to 20 minutes of cooking.

EASY PEASY HAM AND CHEESE CASSEROLE

Servings: 4

This recipe is bound to be a hit with even your pickiest eaters.

1 1/2 cups milk
1 (10.75 ounce) can cream of mushroom soup
2 cups cooked ham, diced
2 cups bowtie pasta, cooked
1 cup green peas, fresh or frozen
1/2 medium yellow onion, chopped
1/2 cup shredded cheese, cheddar or Monterey Jack
1/2 cup bread crumbs (panko-style is preferred)

1.   Preheat oven to 375 degrees F.
2.   Pour milk and soup into 2-quart casserole dish. Stir together to combine. Add in ham, pasta, asparagus, and onion. Stir to combine. Sprinkle with cheese and bread crumbs.
3.   Bake, covered, for 40 minutes. Uncover, and bake an additional 10 minutes or until cheese is golden brown.

SMOTHERED PORK CHOPS

Servings: 4

This is pure comfort food.

4 pork chops
1 can of cream of chicken/celery/or mushroom soup
1/2 package of onion soup mix
2 cup of peas
2 cup of water
1 pouch microwavable rice, or 2 cups cooked

1.   Preheat oven to 375 degrees F.
2.   Combine together all ingredients except for pork chops.
3.   Place pork chops in baking pan. Top with rice mixture.
4.   Bake for 1 hour.

APPLE BUTTER PORK TENDERLOIN

Servings: 4

This needs to marinate overnight, but is definitely worth the wait.

1 (1 lb) pork tenderloin
1/4 teaspoon dried thyme
1/8 teaspoon mustard powder
2 cloves garlic, minced
4 tablespoons soy sauce
4 tablespoons sherry wine

For the Sauce

6 tablespoons apple butter
1 tablespoon sherry wine
1 tablespoon soy sauce
3/4 teaspoon garlic salt, to taste

1.   Combine thyme, garlic, mustard powder, sherry, and soy sauce in a gallon-size zipper lock bag. Add the tenderloin and marinate in the refrigerator for minimum of 4 hours, preferably overnight.
2.   Preheat oven to 400 degrees F.
3.   Remove tenderloin from bag, discard marinade, and place in roasting pan.
4.   Combine the apple butter, sherry, soy sauce, and garlic salt in bowl.
5.   Cover pork with the apple butter mixture.
6.   Place tenderloin into the oven and roast for 30 minutes or until a meat thermometer reads 160 degrees F.

5
Seafood Dishes

EASY SALMON BAKE

Servings: 6

Canned wild salmon makes this dish fast and healthy.

1 1/2 cups elbow macaroni, uncooked
2 (15 ounce) cans salmon, drained
2 (10 ounce) cans cream of chicken soup
3 large carrots, sliced
1 medium yellow onion, chopped
1/2 teaspoon black pepper
1 1/2 cups milk
1 cup cheddar cheese, shredded
1/2 cup bread crumbs

1. Cook macaroni according to package directions. Drain and set aside.
2. Preheat oven to 375 degrees F.
3. In bowl, combine salmon, soup, carrots, macaroni, onion, pepper, and milk. Mix well. Spoon mixture into 9 x 13 baking dish.
4. Sprinkle with cheese and breadcrumbs.
5. Bake, uncovered, for 40 minutes or until light golden brown.

ORANGE MARMALADE MARINATED SALMON

Servings: 4

Very tasty and different salmon recipe.

2/3 cup orange marmalade
1/3 cup rice vinegar
1/3 cup soy sauce
1 teaspoon minced garlic
1 teaspoon grated fresh ginger
1 teaspoon onion powder
1 teaspoon sesame oil
1 teaspoon olive oil
1 pinch chili pepper flakes
black pepper, to taste
2 pounds fresh salmon fillets
fresh sliced scallion (for garnish)

1.   Add all ingredients except for salmon in gallon-size zipper lock plastic bag. Seal and shake to combine. Add salmon, reseal and refrigerate for 1 hour to marinate.
2.   Place salmon in preheated broiler and broil, skin side down, for 5-6 minutes or until center is opaque and fish flakes easily.

FISH BAKED WITH TOMATOES AND POTATOES

....

Servings: 4

This is an easy, one dish seafood dinner.

....

1 1/2 lbs white fish fillets (cod, halibut or haddock)
4 potatoes, peeled and thinly sliced
1/2 medium onion, thinly sliced
1/2 teaspoon salt
1/2 teaspoon pepper
1 (15 ounce) can diced tomatoes, seasoned with garlic and basil
2 tablespoons fresh parsley, chopped
1/2 teaspoon dried oregano

....

1.   Preheat oven to 375 degrees F.
2.   Place fish in baking dish. Top with potatoes, onion, tomatoes, salt, pepper, parsley, and oregano.
3.   Cover with foil and bake for 30 minutes, until potatoes are tender and fish flakes easily.

SOY AND GINGER MAHI MAHI

....

Servings: 4

Enjoy this Asian-inspired dish over rice.

....

2 pounds mahi mahi fillets (4 medium pieces)
2 tablespoons olive oil
2 tablespoons fresh ginger, minced (I use jarred)
1 tablespoon garlic, minced
1 tablespoon fresh lime juice
1/4 cup soy sauce
2 tablespoons honey
2 tablespoons dry red wine
1/8 teaspoon cayenne pepper
Salt and freshly ground black pepper, to taste

....

1.   Combine all ingredients except for fish in a gallon-size zipper close plastic bag. Shake to combine.
2.   Add fish, seal, and place in refrigerator to marinate for at least 4 hours or overnight.
3.   The fish can be cooked either on the grill, in the broiler, or baked in the oven.
4.   To grill or broil, cook for about 4 minutes, turn, and cook for another 2-3 minutes or until fish flakes easily.
5.   To bake, place in baking dish with marinade and cook in 350 degree F oven for 15 minutes or until fish flakes easily.

Note: These are great to freeze and then defrost and cook later.

NEW ENGLAND CLAM CHOWDER

....

Servings: 10

This hearty chowder is rich with potatoes and clams.

....

2 cups skim milk
2 cups 1% milk
2 tablespoons butter, unsalted
3 medium potatoes, peeled and diced
1 medium yellow onion, chopped
2 celery stalks, chopped
1 bag of frozen sweet corn
16 ounces of fresh clams in juice

....

In the slow cooker: Place all ingredients into slow cooker. Cover and cook 2-3 hours on high setting or 4-6 hours on low setting. Onions should be soft and potato should be tender.

On the stovetop: Place all ingredients into large pot. Cover, bring to a boil, reduce heat and simmer for about an hour, until onions are soft and potatoes are tender.

6

Beef Dishes

FAST SHEPHERD'S PIE

Servings: 6

This dish is super quick to make if you use prepared mashed potatoes.

1 pound ground beef
1 cup cheddar cheese, divided
1/2 cup sour cream
3 garlic cloves, minced
4 cup mixed vegetables, thawed if frozen
1 cup beef gravy
2 cups mashed potatoes

1.   Preheat oven to 375 degrees F.
2.   Heat skillet over medium-high heat. Add beef and cook until browned. Drain excess fat.
3.   In a bowl, mix together 1/2 cup cheese, sour cream, and garlic.
4.   Add beef to 9 x 13 baking dish. Top with vegetables and gravy and stir to mix. Spread cheese mixture over top. Cover with mashed potatoes. Sprinkle with remaining cheese.
5.   Bake for 25 minutes or until cheese is melted and dish is heated through.

EASY LASAGNA

Servings: 8

....

1 pound ground beef
1 (9 ounce) package oven-ready lasagna noodles
3 cups spaghetti sauce (jarred or homemade)
1 cup cottage cheese
1 egg
3/4 cup Parmesan cheese
1 teaspoon dried basil
Salt and freshly ground black pepper, to taste
3 cups mozzarella cheese, shredded

....

1.   Preheat oven to 350 degrees F.
2.   Brown meat in skillet and drain.
3.   Mix cottage cheese, egg, Parmesan cheese, basil, salt, and pepper in a bowl.
4.   Spread a little sauce in bottom of 13 x9 baking dish.
5.   Add a layer of lasagna noodles. Spread 1/3 of cottage cheese mixture over noodles. Spread 1/3 ground beef over cheese mixture, Spoon 1 cup of sauce over ground beef. Sprinkle 1 cup mozzarella cheese over sauce. Repeat layers 2 more times, ending with a layer of mozzarella cheese on top.
6.   Bake in oven, covered for 45 minutes. Remove cover and cook for an additional 15 minutes or until heated through and cheese is light golden brown.

PEPPERONI PIZZA BAKE

Servings: 6
This super quick dish is a kid pleaser.

1 can Pillsbury Grands refrigerated buttermilk biscuits
1 cup pizza sauce
2 cups mozzarella cheese, shredded
16 pepperoni slices

1.   Preheat oven to 375 degrees F.
2.   Cut biscuits into pieces. Mix together with sauce and 1 cup of cheese.
3.   Spread into 8-inch square baking dish. Top with remaining cheese and pepperoni slices.
4.   Bake for about 25 minutes, until cheese is golden brown and bubbly.

SLOW COOKER TORTELLINI AND MEATBALLS

Servings: 4

1 (1.5 pound) bag frozen Italian style meatballs
1 (1.5 pound) bag frozen cheese tortellini
1 (20 ounce) jar marinara sauce (or other favorite sauce)
1 (8 ounce) can tomato sauce
1 teaspoon dried oregano
1 teaspoon dried basil
Freshly ground black pepper, to taste
1 cup water
2 cups mozzarella cheese, shredded
1/3 cup Parmesan cheese

In a slow cooker: Combine all ingredients except cheeses in slow cooker. Cover and cook on low for 6 hours. Serve topped with cheeses.

On the stove top: Add all ingredients except cheeses to large saucepan. Cook over medium heat, covered, for about 30 minutes, until meatballs are heated through. Serve topped with cheeses.

SWISS STEAK

This is simple to put together and the meat comes out very tender.

1 pound round or cube steak, cut into pieces
1 (15 ounce) can diced tomatoes
½ package of dry onion soup mix
½ package dry brown gravy mix

In the oven: Place all ingredients in baking dish and bake for 90 minutes at 350 degrees F.

In a slow cooker: Place all ingredients in slow cooker. Cover and cook on low for 6-7 hours or high for 4-5 hours.

EASY PIZZA-STYLE MINI MEATLOAF CUPS

Servings: 12

1 egg, beaten
½ cup pizza sauce plus extra for topping
¼ cup bread crumbs, Italian-seasoned
1 teaspoon basil
1 teaspoon oregano
Salt and freshly ground black pepper, to taste
1 ½ pounds ground beef
1 ½ cups mozzarella cheese, shredded

1.	Preheat oven to 375 degrees F. Lightly coat muffin tins with cooking spray.
2.	In a bowl, mix together egg, pizza sauce, bread crumbs, basil, oregano, salt, and pepper. Add ground beef and mix well.
3.	Divide mixture evenly into muffin tins. Press down in center of beef mixture to make indent in center. Fill center with shredded cheese.
4.	Bake for 15 minutes or until meat is cooked through.
5.	Serve topped with additional sauce and cheese.

BEEF AND BEAN CORNBREAD SKILLET DINNER

Servings: 4

1 pound ground beef
1 packet taco seasoning mix
½ cup water
1 (15 ounce) can black beans, rinsed and drained
1 (15 ounce) can corn, drained
1 package cornbread mix
1 egg, lightly beaten
2/3 cup milk

1.   Preheat oven to 400 degrees F.
2.   Heat cast iron skillet over medium heat. Brown beef and drain. Add taco seasoning and water and cook over medium heat for about 5 minutes until most of water is absorbed. Add black beans and corn and stir. Remove from heat.
3.   In a bowl, mix together cornbread mix, milk, and egg until just combined. Pour over ground beef in skillet.
4.   Bake in oven for 20-25 minutes, until cornbread is golden brown.

CHEESEBURGER MACARONI AND CHEESE

....

Servings: 5

You can get this hearty mac and cheese meal on the table in less than 30 minutes.

....

1 pound ground beef
1 package Velveeta Cheesy Skillet Dinner
2 cups water (as called for on skillet dinner box)
1/4 cup barbecue sauce
2 tablespoons Worcestershire sauce
1 tablespoon onion powder
1 cup cheddar cheese, shredded

....

1. Heat large skillet over medium heat. Add ground beef and cook, stirring, until browned.
2. Prepare Velveeta Skillet Dinner according to package directions.
3. Stir in cheese sauce, BBQ sauce, Worcestershire sauce, and onion powder. Pour into baking dish and sprinkle with shredded cheese.
4. Bake in preheated 350 degree F. oven for 5 minutes or until cheese is melted.

Broccoli and Beef

Servings: 4

1/4 cup all-purpose flour
1 (10.5 ounce) can beef broth
2 tablespoons white sugar
2 tablespoons soy sauce
1 pound boneless round steak, cut into bite size pieces
1/4 teaspoon chopped fresh ginger root
1 clove garlic, minced
4 cups chopped fresh broccoli

1. In a small bowl, combine flour, broth, sugar, and soy sauce. Stir until sugar and flour are dissolved.
2. In a large skillet over high heat, cook and stir beef 2 to 4 minutes, or until browned. Stir in broth mixture, ginger, garlic, and broccoli. Bring to a boil, then reduce heat. Simmer 5 to 10 minutes, or until sauce thickens.
3. Serve over rice.

MEATBALL SUB CASSEROLE

Servings: 6

1 (16 ounce) package frozen Italian style meatballs
1 loaf French bread, sliced
8 ounces ricotta cheese
¼ cup Parmesan cheese
3 cloves garlic, minced
1 tablespoon Italian seasoning
1 jar pasta sauce
2 cups mozzarella cheese, shredded

1.   Cook meatballs according to package directions.
2.   Spread bread slices in bottom of 9 x 13 baking pan.
3.   In a bowl, mix ricotta cheese, Parmesan cheese, garlic, and Italian seasoning. Spread mixture over bread slices. Place meatballs on top. Pour sauce over meatballs. Top with shredded cheese.
4.   Bake in 350 degree F oven for 30 minutes, until cheese is melted and bubbly.

MOROCCAN-STYLE MEATBALLS

Servings: 4

1 tablespoon olive oil
1 package frozen meatballs (beef or chicken)
1 yellow onion, sliced
½ cup dried apricots, chopped
1 teaspoon cinnamon
1 (15 ounce) can chopped tomatoes
½ cup water
1 can black olives, pitted
1 (15 ounce) can chickpeas, drained
2 garlic cloves, minced
4 eggs
¼ cup sliced almonds
½ cup fresh coriander, chopped

1.   Heat olive oil in large saucepan over medium heat. Add meatballs and cook for 10 minutes, turning occasionally, until heated through. Add onions and cook for an additional 3-4 minutes.
2.   Add apricots, cinnamon, tomatoes, water, olives, chickpeas, and garlic. Simmer for 10-15 minutes.
3.   Make 4 hollows in sauce. Break in eggs. Cover and cook for 5-6 minutes over low heat until eggs are set.
4.   Serve sprinkled with almonds and coriander.

Note: Serve over couscous.

7

Pasta and Vegetable Dishes

BAKED MACARONI AND CHEESE

Servings: 6-8

 1 (1 pound) box elbow macaroni
1 pound extra-sharp cheddar cheese, shredded
4 tablespoons butter, cut into pieces
2 eggs, beaten
1 (12 ounce) can evaporated milk
1 teaspoon Dijon mustard
Salt and freshly ground black pepper, to taste
½ cup bread crumbs (Panko-style preferred)

1.   Preheat oven to 350 degrees F.
2.   Cook macaroni according to package directions.
3.   Spray 9 x 13 casserole dish with cooking spray.
4.   Add all ingredients except for bread crumbs to casserole dish and mix well to combine.
Sprinkle with bread crumbs.
5.   Bake for 30 minutes or until golden brown.

SOUTHWESTERN-STYLE TORTELLINI CASSEROLE

....

Servings: 4

....

1 (15 ounce) can black beans, rinsed and drained
1 (10 ounce) package fresh cheese tortellini
1 (4 ounce can) green chilies, diced
1 (15 ounce can) diced tomatoes
 1 small zucchini, sliced
½ teaspoon cayenne pepper
½ teaspoon cumin
1 ½ cups sour cream, regular or low-fat
¼ cup lime juice
2 cups Monterey Jack cheese, shredded
½ cup black olives, sliced
¾ cup green onion, chopped
¼ cup cilantro, chopped

....

1.   Preheat oven to 350 degrees F.
2.   Spray 1 ½-2 quart casserole dish with cooking spray.
3.   In a bowl, mix together beans, tortellini, chilies, diced tomatoes, zucchini, cayenne, and cumin. Pour into casserole dish.
4.   In a bowl, mix together sour cream and lime juice. Spread over tortellini mixture.
5.   Sprinkle with cheese, olives, green onion, and cilantro.
6.   Cover and bake for 30 minutes. Uncover and cook for another 20-25 minutes, or until cheese is golden brown and bubbly.

VEGETABLE RAMEN

Servings: 4

Ramen noodles cook very quickly and make a simple, yet satisfying meal.

5 cups chicken or vegetable broth
1 bag frozen mixed vegetables
3 packages ramen noodles
1 tablespoon sesame oil
2 tablespoons soy sauce

1.   Pour broth into saucepan and bring to a boil. Add frozen vegetables and cook for 4-5 minutes, until vegetables are heated through. Add ramen noodles, 1 seasoning packet (discard other two), sesame oil, and soy sauce. Cook for 1-2 minutes, until noodles are soft.
2.   Serve hot.

EASY SPINACH QUICHE

Servings: 6-8

1 prepared pie crust
1 tablespoon olive oil
1 medium onion, chopped
1 (10 ounce) package frozen spinach, thawed
5 eggs, lightly beaten
¾ cup Swiss cheese, grated
Salt and freshly ground black pepper to taste

1.	Preheat oven to 350 degrees F.
2.	Heat oil in skillet over medium high heat. Add onion and sauté for 4-5 minutes. Add spinach and cook for 5-6 minutes, until most liquid evaporates.
3.	In a bowl, mix together eggs and cheese. Stir in spinach-onion mixture. Season with salt and pepper. Pour into pie crust.
4.	Bake for 40-45 minutes or until toothpick inserted in center comes out clean.

From the Author

Thank you for reading *Dump Dinners: Amazingly Easy and Delicious Dump Recipes.* I sincerely hope that you found this book informative and helpful and that it helps you to create delicious meals for your family with little stress or fuss.

Happy cooking!

Index

More Bestselling Titles from Dylanna Press

Mason Jar Meals by Dylanna Press

Mason jar meals are a fun and practical way to take your meals on the go. Mason jars are an easy way to prepare individual servings, so whether you're cooking for one, two, or a whole crowd, these fun, make-ahead meals will work.

Includes More than 50 Recipes and Full-Color Photos
In this book, you'll find a wide variety of recipes including all kinds of salads, as well as hot meal ideas such as mini chicken pot pies and lasagna in a jar. Also included are mouth-watering desserts such as strawberry shortcake, apple pie, and s'mores.

The recipes are easy to prepare and don't require any special cooking skills. So what are you waiting for? Grab your Mason jars and start preparing these gorgeous and tasty dishes!

The Inflammation Diet by Dylanna Press

Beat Pain, Slow Aging, and Reduce Risk of Heart Disease with the Inflammation Diet.

Inflammation has been called the "silent killer" and it has been linked to a wide variety of illnesses including heart disease, arthritis, diabetes, chronic pain, autoimmune disorders, and cancer.

Often, the root of chronic inflammation is in the foods we eat.

The Inflammation Diet: Complete Guide to Beating Pain and Inflammation will show you how, by making simple changes to your diet, you can greatly reduce inflammation in your body and reduce your symptoms and lower your risk of chronic disease.

The book includes a complete plan for eliminating inflammation and implementing an anti-inflammatory diet:

- Overview of inflammation and the body's immune response – what can trigger it and why chronic inflammation is harmful
- The link between diet and inflammation
- Inflammatory foods to avoid
- Anti-inflammatory foods to add to your diet to beat pain and inflammation
- Over 50 delicious inflammation diet recipes
- A 14-day meal plan

Take charge of your health and implement the inflammation diet to lose weight, slow the aging process, eliminate chronic pain, and reduce the likelihood and symptoms of chronic disease.

Learn how to heal your body from within through diet.

106